THE LAST YEARS OF
NORTH WEST STEAM

BEN BROOKSBANK
PETER TUFFREY

GREAT N ORTHERN

ACKNOWLEDGEMENTS

In compiling this book I am grateful for the assistance received from the following people: Ben Brooksbank, Doug Brown, David Burrill, David Clay, Peter Crangle, David Dippie, Peter Jary, David Joy, Hugh Parkin, Bill Reed.

Gratitude should also be expressed to my son Tristram for his general help and encouragement throughout the course of the project.

PHOTOGRAPHS

Every effort has been made to gain permission to use the photographs in this book. If you feel you have not been contacted please let me know: petertuffrey@rocketmail.com.

Great Northern Books
PO Box 1380, Bradford, BD5 5FB
www.greatnorthernbooks.co.uk

© Peter Tuffrey 2019

Every effort has been made to acknowledge correctly and contact the copyright holders of material in this book. Great Northern Books Ltd apologises for any unintentional errors or omissions, which should be notified to the publisher.

ISBN: 978-1-912101-11-5

Design and layout: David Burrill

CIP Data
A catalogue for this book is available from the British Library

INTRODUCTION

North West England was the cradle of steam railways, nurturing the Liverpool & Manchester Railway which was the first inter-city line in the country. Nearly 140 years later when the era of steam traction drew to a close, the region became a safe haven for surviving locomotives and a place of considerable interest for the photographers of the day.

Although plateways (an early form of railway) had been in use from the late 18th century, these were often short and utilised the power of horses to convey the products of industry — usually coal. The first step towards a modern railway was made by the Stockton & Darlington Railway in 1825 with the opening of the line from Witton Park Colliery, north-west of Shildon, and Stockton via Darlington. A mixture of steam and horse power was used to convey coal and passengers along the 25 miles of iron rails and, after initial teething problems, proved quite successful.

In the early 1820s plans for a railway line from Liverpool to Manchester were formulated to reduce the monopoly canal companies held on the transportation of the raw materials from the ports and finished products leaving the inland factories. The Bill for the line was passed in 1826 and construction commenced soon afterwards under George Stephenson and Joseph Locke.

There were major works at the Liverpool end of the line, with the route having to penetrate the bedrock near Edge Hill and a tunnel was created from there to Wapping Dock, measuring over one mile in length. Close to Manchester, the bog at Chat Moss was crossed, requiring much work to create stable foundations.

The line opened amidst great celebrations on 15th September 1830, with the Duke of Wellington — then Prime Minister — in attendance. Sadly, the day was marred by the death of MP for Liverpool William Huskisson, who was run over by a train travelling in the opposite direction after he had alighted while his own train was stopped to take on water.

The Liverpool & Manchester Railway went on to be successful in competing against the canals and also benefitted from the transportation of passengers, which was a secondary consideration. From the outset steam locomotives were employed successfully.

With the example set by the Stockton & Darlington and Liverpool & Manchester Railways, several other schemes were able to find backers. The Warrington & Newton Railway made a junction with the L&MR in 1831, followed by the Wigan Branch Railway in 1832. The latter became part of the North Union Railway when the company was formed through amalgamation with the Wigan & Preston Railway in 1834.

As local railway lines proved their worth, the connection of towns and cities further afield became much more realistic. The Grand Junction Railway was formed in 1832 to connect Birmingham with Liverpool and Manchester via the existing Warrington & Newton Railway. The scheme was accepted in 1833 with George Stephenson and Joseph Locke again employed to oversee construction, which was completed in 1837. The London & Birmingham Railway was ready for traffic during the following year, allowing travel between the North West and the capital.

The difficult route over the Pennines was first tackled by the Manchester & Leeds Railway and the line opened in 1839. Following on in stages between 1841 and 1845 was the Sheffield, Ashton-under-Lyne and Manchester Railway (subsequently Manchester, Sheffield & Lincolnshire Railway).

The ultimate goal for railway companies in the North West at this time was the connection of London with Glasgow. Laying the final sections of line were the Lancaster & Carlisle Railway (operational from late 1846) and the Caledonian Railway, which opened the route from Carlisle to Glasgow in February 1848.

With the pieces in place, the larger companies were able to monopolise sections of the North West. The London & North Western Railway, which later became one of the largest companies in the world, was formed from the GJR, L&BR and Manchester & Birmingham Railway (opened from Crewe to Manchester in 1840) during 1846. In the following year the M&LR was just one of the companies amalgamated to produce the Lancashire & Yorkshire Railway which went on to challenge the LNWR in the area through leases and acquisitions of strategically important lines.

As with the canal companies some years earlier, the LNWR and L&YR held an advantageous position over passengers and businesses alike. In the early 1860s, the Cheshire Lines Committee was founded with backing from the Great Northern Railway and Manchester, Sheffield & Lincolnshire Railway, later also the Midland Railway, to challenge the established dominant companies in the North West. This was mainly done through the promotion and construction of a new line between Manchester and Liverpool (opened 1873), followed by a line from Manchester to Chester (1874) and from Liverpool to Southport (1884).

With the LNWR, L&YR and CLC operating both passenger and freight trains throughout the North West, there was a fascinating array of motive power and traffic to be seen by enthusiasts. This fact was not altered by the Grouping of 1923, when the LNWR and L&YR were constituents of the London Midland & Scottish Railways and the CLC used motive power from the London & North Eastern Railway, or Nationalisation in 1948. In this instance the area came under the jurisdiction of the London Midland Region of British Railways.

The formation of British Railways' regions perhaps did little to alter the autonomy of the particular areas, although Scotland was unified. The London Midland Region consisted of the West Coast Main Line and Midland Main Line from London to Carlisle, in addition to the two lines between Manchester and Liverpool and several other local systems that had previously been operated by the LMSR.

Locomotives and rolling stock types continued to be those employed before Nationalisation, but there were later new types introduced by BR. The war years had kept many older locomotives, which would have otherwise been withdrawn, in service, and these had to be replaced. Whilst countries on the continent moved over to electric and diesel traction, BR

favoured perpetuating the use of steam locomotives to meet the immediate needs of the network. Nearly 1000 new engines were erected up to the late 1950s and these were employed across the country, with many finding homes in the North West. These included the Class 7 'Britannia' Pacifics, Class 5 4-6-0s, Class 4 2-6-0s and 9F 2-10-0s, amongst others. Large numbers of freight locomotives had also been built for the War Department during the war and these 'Austerity' 2-8-0s also found their way to depots in the area.

Yet, the most familiar engines at work in the North West were the designs of Fowler and Stanier of the LMSR. Both of these Chief Mechanical Engineers had adopted a policy of standardisation in order to keep reliability high and maintenance costs low. Fowler produced the robust 4F Class 0-6-0 and the 'Royal Scot' 4-6-0s during his tenure and both worked in the North West on freight services and express passenger trains respectively. Stanier's appointment was made in the early 1930s in order to further improve the LMSR stock. His first major design was the 'Princess Royal' Pacific, followed by the 'Jubilee' and Class 5 4-6-0s, as well as the 8F 2-8-0 freight class. Very large numbers of the 4-6-0s and 2-8-0s were eventually produced and the 'Princess Royal' design was developed into the 'Coronation' Pacific Class which became the principal motive power for the top expresses running on the WCML.

Adding variation to the scene during the 1950s and into the early 1960s was ex-LNWR 0-8-0s, along with some ex-L&YR designs. Ex-Great Central Railway classes were present in Manchester, Liverpool and Northwich during the same period for working the old CLC lines. On the odd occasion LNER designs from Sir Nigel Gresley and Edward Thompson could be seen travelling towards the coastal resorts of Blackpool and others with special trains run for holidaymakers during the summer months. Gresley A3 Pacifics often worked from Edinburgh into Carlisle with expresses on the Waverley route. Locomotives of the Great Western Railway also passed into the area with passenger services to Crewe and Chester, in addition to freight trains to there and the ports at Birkenhead.

The Mersey Docks & Harbour Board operated a stud of small locomotives for shunting freight around the extensive yards around Liverpool. Collieries of the

Lancashire coalfield also used steam shunting engines for sorting wagons right up to the 1980s.

Drawing images from several sources, the *Last Years of North West Steam* illustrates the varied steam scene in the North West of England from the post–Nationalisation years to the end of steam in 1968. The southern border of the collection has been set at Crewe and Chester and in the north at Carlisle, covering the diverse landscape between – from the great locomotive workshops at Crewe and Gorton, to the passenger stations at Chester and Liverpool and sidings at Farington, Lostock Hall and Aintree. The imposing, yet striking, surroundings of the Lake District frame several images included here of locomotives working on the WCML between Tebay and Penrith, whilst further north at Carlisle the varied scene of this important railway centre has been well illustrated. A number of images captured at engine depots are included, such as those at Carnforth, Newton Heath, Heaton Mersey, Patricroft and Stockport.

With this collection of photographs, the author hopes that the memories of steam are rekindled for those who lived through the final years and those younger get a good indication of the halcyon days, long since passed, and hopefully never forgotten.

Peter Tuffrey
Doncaster, December 2018

Above ALDERLEY EDGE
South of Alderley Edge station, Hughes 'Crab' Class 2-6-0 no. 42920 is seen on 28th July 1951 with an up Manchester to Plymouth holiday express. Photograph by B.W.L. Brooksbank.

Opposite above AINTREE SHED
Nestled in a complex group of lines just to the south west of Aintree Racecourse was Aintree locomotive shed. The Liverpool, Ormskirk & Preston Railway (backed by the East Lancashire Railway) was the first to forge a way through the area in 1849, joining the Liverpool & Bury Railway south of Aintree before terminating at Liverpool Exchange station. Both lines were subsequently taken over by the Lancashire & Yorkshire Railway, which, in the mid-1860s, decided to bypass the centre of Liverpool and reach the docks from the north. A route was constructed from the Liverpool & Bury Railway line at Fazakerley Junction near Kirkby, running west to Litherland where the line curved south to Seaforth and provided access to the docks — later Alexandra and Gladstone Docks. Aintree shed was erected by the L&YR on the north side of the line in 1886, likely to serve the large sidings built around the same time, and the building had eight roads, with a repair shop, turntable (50 ft) and coal stage. Moving west out of the shed yard on 20th August 1948 is Fowler 7F 0-8-0 no. 49592. Photograph by B.W.L. Brooksbank.

Opposite below AINTREE SIDINGS
View west from alongside the North Mersey line at Aintree on 12th June 1959 as ex-War Department 2-8-0 no. 90557 trundles past with a Class F freight train. This site was previously occupied by Ford station, which was the only one on the route and open just for the Grand National race meeting. Photograph by B.W.L. Brooksbank.

ALLERTON

Stanier Class 8F 2-8-0 no. 48723 passes under Greenhill Road bridge — between West Allerton and Allerton stations, Liverpool — with a freight train on 29th February 1968. Allocated to Heaton Mersey at this time, the engine moved to Lostock Hall in May and was condemned there in August. Photograph by David Christie.

Above ASHTON

Approaching Ashton (Charlestown) station on 26th July 1951 is Stanier 4P Class 2-6-4T no. 42645. The engine is heading a local service, perhaps from Manchester Exchange to Huddersfield. Photograph by B.W.L. Brooksbank.

Below BACUP

Opened in late 1852, Bacup station was the terminus for a line from Bury. A second route to the town from Rochdale was laid by the L&YR and opened in 1881, shortly after a new station at Bacup was completed. This facility is illustrated here in mid-1963, some three years before closure. Photograph by B.W.L. Brooksbank.

Above BAGULEY

Hughes 'Crab' Class 2-6-0 no. 42924 has a Class H freight service and is travelling westward towards Baguley station on 5th May 1965. Photograph by B.W.L. Brooksbank.

Below BAGULEY

View east from Butcher Lane bridge, Baguley, again on 5th May 1965, as Ivatt 4MT 2-6-0 no. 43048 approaches with a westbound mineral train. Photograph by B.W.L. Brooksbank.

Above **BAGULEY STATION**
The closure of Baguley station in November 1964 was 18 months away when Stanier 8F no. 48249 was recorded travelling westward with a limestone train from Peak Forest to ICI Winnington, Northwich. Photograph by B.W.L. Brooksbank.

Below **BAMBER BRIDGE STATION**
A quiet scene has been captured here at Bamber Bridge station, from the level crossing on the B6258, on 20th August 1963. Photograph by B.W.L. Brooksbank.

Above BIDSTON
Iron ore traffic between Bidston Dock and John Summers Steelworks, Shotton, was a regular duty for locally based BR Standard Class 9Fs. No. 92046 heads such a train at Bidston during 1960. Photograph by Rev. J. David Benson courtesy A1 Steam Trust.

Below BICKERSHAW & ABRAM STATION
Operational between 1st April 1884 and 2nd November 1964, Bickershaw & Abram station (illustrated here on 20th August 1963) was located on the line from Glazebrook to Wigan. Photograph by B.W.L. Brooksbank.

Above BASSENTHWAITE LAKE STATION

Ivatt Class 2MT 2-6-0 no. 46449 heads the 10.15 Manchester Victoria to Workington service on the Cockermouth, Keswick and Penrith line on Saturday, 11th August 1951. Photograph by B.W.L. Brooksbank.

Below BIRKENHEAD MOLLINGTON STREET SHED

The Great Western Railway and LNWR established joint shed facilities at Birkenhead in 1878, opening two eight-track depots south of Birkenhead Town station. The site is depicted here on 20th June 1948 with both ex-LMSR and ex-GWR engines in the yard. Photograph by B.W.L. Brooksbank.

Above **BLACKBURN STATION**
Opened in 1846 by the Blackburn & Preston Railway, Blackburn station was later enlarged by the L&YR in the late 1880s to cope with growing traffic requirements. At the time of this picture — 5th May 1965 — Blackburn station had lost several services through line closures in the local area, contributing here to the abandoned air of the station. Some have since been restored and the station was modernised in the early 2000s which unfortunately saw the demolition of the train sheds. Photograph by B.W.L. Brooksbank.

Below **BLACKBURN STATION**
Stanier Class 5 4-6-0 no. 45095 hauls a mixed freight train eastward through Blackburn station on 8th May 1965. Photograph by B.W.L. Brooksbank.

Above **BLACKPOOL CENTRAL STATION**
At the head of the 13.45 express from Blackpool Central to Bradford is Stanier 'Jubilee' Class 4-6-0 no. 45565 *Victoria*. Captured during October 1964, the locomotive was allocated to Bradford Low Moor shed and would be withdrawn from there in January 1967. Photograph by Bill Reed.

Below **BLACKPOOL CENTRAL SHED**
A distance to the south of Blackpool Central station, the locomotive shed sat on the eastern side of the main lines. Stanier Class 5 4-6-0 no. 45051 is seen there over the pits during October 1964. Photograph by Bill Reed.

Above BLACKPOOL CENTRAL SHED

View from the ramped coal stage at Blackpool Central shed to the turntable line, on which stands Stanier 'Jubilee' Class 4-6-0 no. 45593 *Kolhapur* during October 1964. The engine was a recent addition to the ranks at Patricroft depot. Photograph by Bill Reed.

Below BLACKPOOL NORTH SHED

Located off a short spur from the main running lines, Blackpool North shed was erected by the Preston & Wyre Joint Railway in 1886 and consisted of three roads with turntable and coal stage. Standing outside the building is long-term resident Stanier 4P Class 2-6-4T no. 42638. Photograph by Bill Reed.

Above BLACKROD STATION

Stanier 4P Class 2-6-4T no. 42662 was two weeks into a six-week allocation to Accrington when pictured departing Blackrod station with an up local service on 16th April 1962. The engine moved on to Southport and was withdrawn from there in December 1964. Photograph by B.W.L. Brooksbank.

Below BLACKROD STATION

View south at Blackrod station as Stanier 'Jubilee' Class 4-6-0 no. 45705 *Seahorse* approaches with the 16.15 Manchester to Preston stopping train on 16th April 1962. Photograph by B.W.L. Brooksbank.

BOLD COLLIERY

Located to the south east of St Helens, Bold Colliery was operational from the mid-1870s to November 1985. Even though BR had abandoned steam locomotives, the NCB continued using engines until the mid-1980s. Here, on 13th May 1981 NCB no. 7 *Robert* is shown in the colliery yard. Photograph by John Law.

Above **BOLD COLLIERY**

NCB no. 7 *Robert* shunts empty hopper wagons on 13th May 1981. The locomotive was built for the War Department by Hudswell Clarke in 1943 and was later purchased by the NCB. Initially working in the Midlands, no. 7 moved to Bold Colliery in 1978 and was employed there until 1982 when sold for preservation; the engine is currently being restored. Photograph by John Law.

Below **BOLTON SHED**

A group of forlorn engines (perhaps withdrawn) stand in the yard at Bolton shed. Fowler 7F 0-8-0 no. 49662 is the focus of this shot and was at the depot from December 1957 to May 1959 when condemned. Photograph by Bill Reed.

Above **BOLTON TRINITY STREET STATION**
Standard Class 2MT 2-6-2T no. 84014 is lightly loaded with just a brake van at the north end of Trinity Street station, Bolton, on 20th August 1963. The locomotive was allocated to Bolton shed at this time (February 1959-December 1964) and had been based in the area from new in September 1953. No. 84014 survived until December 1965. Photograph by B.W.L. Brooksbank.

Opposite page **BOLTON TRINITY STREET STATION**
The Manchester & Bolton Railway opened Trinity Street station (as Bolton) on 29th May 1838 as the terminus for the company's line from Salford. Only a few years later the route was extended to Preston and the station was subsequently rebuilt. Depicted at the south end of the station on 1st March 1968 is Stanier Class 5 no. 45290. Photograph by David Christie.

Above BOLTON TRINITY STREET STATION
A down iron ore train is headed through Bolton Trinity Street by Hughes 'Crab' no. 42727 on 20th August 1963. Photograph by B.W.L. Brooksbank.

Opposite page BOLTON SHED
Stanier Class 5 no. 44802 reverses under signals near Bolton shed (south of the station) on 1st March 1968. Photograph by David Christie.

Below BOLTON TRINITY STREET STATION
A local service to Manchester Victoria stands at the up platform at Bolton Trinity Street station behind Standard Class 4MT no. 75047 on 3rd May 1965. Photograph by B.W.L. Brooksbank.

Above BRUNSWICK SHED

Located alongside the Cheshire Lines Committee's route to Liverpool Central, Brunswick shed served the large goods station of the same name just to the north. Here, ex-GCR D9 Class 4-4-0 no. 2314 is viewed on the eastern side of the depot at the coal stage, with the turntable in the background, on 28th June 1948; the vantage point was the footbridge from Herculaneum station on the Liverpool Overhead Railway. Photograph by B.W.L. Brooksbank.

Below BOLTON-LE-SANDS

The 16.35 from Liverpool Exchange to Glasgow Central speeds through Bolton-le-Sands station behind 'Jubilee' no. 45717 *Dauntless* on 10th September 1962. Photograph by B.W.L. Brooksbank.

Above BURNLEY BARRACKS STATION

A quiet scene captured at Burnley Barracks station on 22nd September 1962. The station remains open today as a request stop. Photograph by B.W.L. Brooksbank.

Below BURY BOLTON STREET STATION

View north at Bury Bolton Street station on 20th August 1963, with two DMUs at the platforms. The station was rebuilt in 1991 as a transport interchange. Photograph by B.W.L. Brooksbank.

Above and Below BOOTLE, REGENT ROAD

Mersey Docks & Harbour Board 0-6-0ST locomotive no. 1 (below) has been captured working north along Regent Road, Bootle, during 1964, whilst an unidentified stablemate travels in the opposite direction (above). Both photographs by John Arnott Brown courtesy A1 Steam Trust.

Above and Below BROMBOROUGH STATION

Two views captured during the late 1950s/early 1960s at Bromborough station on the Chester to Birkenhead line. Above, ex-GWR Collett '2884' Class 2-8-0 no. 3815 heads a northbound freight and below, Stanier 8F no. 48457 has an up freight. Both pictures by Rev. J. David Benson courtesy A1 Steam Trust.

Above BURNLEY ROSE GROVE SHED

Three Stanier 8F Class 2-8-0s and a Stanier 4-6-0 are serviced near the turntable at Rose Grove shed, Burnley, on 29th July 1966. On the left is no. 48448, which was allocated to the depot at this time, the centre engine is unidentifiable and the far 8F is no. 48211, another resident. Photograph by B.W.L. Brooksbank.

Below BURSCOUGH BRIDGE JUNCTION

View east from Moss Lane Bridge, Burscough, to Burscough Bridge Junction on 26th August 1964. This was the point where the Manchester-Wigan-Southport line connected with the Liverpool-Preston route via two spurs; these were removed in the early 1970s/early 1980s respectively. No. 45409 is at the head of the 17.10 service from Manchester Victoria to Southport. Photograph by B.W.L. Brooksbank.

Above CARLISLE CANAL SHED
Gresley A3 no. 60068 *Sir Visto* is seen with 'The Waverley' headboard at Carlisle Canal shed in the early 1960s. Photograph by Bill Reed.

Below CARLISLE CANAL SHED
Holmes J36 Class 0-6-0 no. 65312 was one of three class members with long-term allocations to Canal depot under BR. Photograph by Bill Reed.

Above CARLISLE KINGMOOR SHED

Stanier 4P Class 2-6-4T no. 42440 only had a brief allocation to Carlisle Kingmoor shed, spanning 15 months from March 1958 to June 1959. Photograph by Bill Reed.

Below CARLISLE KINGMOOR SHED

At the north end of Kingmoor depot's eight-track shed is Fowler 'Patriot' Class no. 45521 *Rhyl*. The engine was based at Wigan Springs Branch depot at this time. Photograph by Bill Reed.

Above CARLISLE KINGMOOR SHED
Ready to take on water at Kingmoor before working the Carlisle-Leeds portion of 'The Waverley' express is 'Britannia' Class Pacific no. 70054 *Dornoch Firth*. Photograph by Bill Reed.

Below CARLISLE KINGMOOR SHED
Few Stanier 4P Class engines were allocated to Kingmoor under BR. No. 42542 was one of three on the roster, lasting from March 1958 to March 1960. Photograph by Bill Reed.

Above CARLISLE KINGMOOR SHED

Seen near Kingmoor depot's turntable, which was at the southern end of the site on the east side of the main lines, is Standard Class 9F no. 92137, 22nd June 1966. Photograph by David Christie.

Below CARLISLE KINGMOOR SHED

Stanier Class 5 no. 44852 moves forward to Carlisle Kingmoor shed for servicing on 22nd June 1966. The engine had 15 months left in traffic at Leeds Holbeck. Photograph by David Christie.

Above CARLISLE KINGMOOR SHED

Another Class 5 at Kingmoor on 22nd June 1966 was no. 44679, which is on the 70 ft turntable. Photograph by David Christie.

Below CARLISLE KINGMOOR SHED

View south from Etterby Road bridge as 8F no. 48709 approaches Kingmoor shed on 22nd June 1966. Note 'LMS 1940' on the bridge brickwork left of the engine. Photograph by David Christie.

Above CARLISLE STATION
Stanier 'Coronation' Class Pacific no. 46238 *City of Carlisle* adds a little colour to the drab surroundings of Carlisle station on 27th June 1964. From June 1958 the engine had been one of a number of class members that were decorated in LMSR-style maroon livery during the BR era. Photograph by David Christie.

Below CARLISLE STATION
Three engines are viewed at the south end of Carlisle station on 27th June 1964. On the left is Stanier Class 5 no. 45194, in the middle is 'Britannia' no. 70038 *Robin Hood* and right is Standard Class 5 no. 73059. Photograph by David Christie.

Above **CARLISLE STATION**

Erected at Derby Works in December 1927, Fowler 4P Class 2-6-4T no. 42301 was in service for nearly 36 years; the last three were spent at Upperby and Kingmoor. The engine is at Carlisle station on 11th May 1959 when a resident of Oxenholme. Photograph by Bill Reed.

Below **CARLISLE STATION**

Fowler 3F Class 0-6-0T no. 47667 is engaged in freight movement as part of the engine's role of station pilot at Carlisle on 27th June 1964. No. 47667 left Camden shed for Carlisle April 1958 and was at both Kingmoor and Upperby before moving on in September 1966. Photograph by David Christie.

Above CARLISLE STATION

BR Standard Class 7 'Britannia' Pacific no. 70025 *Western Star* has been stopped at Carlisle station whilst working a van train on 27th June 1964. The locomotive was erected at Crewe Works in September 1952 and was employed for several years in South Wales at Cardiff Canton depot before moving to Aston shed in September 1961. From there the engine switched to Crewe North, Crewe South and Llandudno Junction before arriving at Carlisle Kingmoor in September 1966. At the end of 1967 *Western Star* was one of several 'Britannias' condemned at the depot. Photograph by David Christie.

Opposite above CARLISLE STATION

Introduced in 1927 by the London Midland & Scottish Railway, the 'Thames-Clyde Express' ran on the ex-Midland Railway route between London St Pancras and Glasgow St Enoch stations. After the war, the northbound and southbound trains departed at 09.50 and 09.15 respectively, taking just over 10 hours to travel the 420 (approx.) miles. The Carlisle to Leeds portion ran non-stop and Fowler 'Royal Scot' no. 46133 *The Green Howards* is ready to begin this section on 22nd July 1953. Photograph by Geoff Warnes.

Opposite below CARLISLE STATION

W.P. Reid updated his Class B 0-6-0 design just before the end of 1914 with the introduction of superheated boilers and larger cylinders for new classmembers. Over 100 were erected by Cowlairs Works and the North British Locomotive Company up to 1921. No. 64608 was sent into traffic from the latter (as North British Railway no. 302) during December 1919 and was part of a group that featured a higher boiler pressure — 175 lb per sq. in. compared to 165 lb per sq. in. of earlier locomotives. No. 64608 is presented here at Carlisle station on 11th August 1960 ready to depart with the 18.13 slow train to Hawick (arrival expected to be 19.47). Photograph by B.W.L. Brooksbank.

Above CARLISLE LONDON ROAD JUNCTION
Stanier Class 5 no. 45212 comes off the Carlisle Avoiding Line to rejoin the main line to Leeds on 12th August 1967. The bridge in the background is carrying lines from Crown Street Goods station (ex-London & North Western Railway) and the banked line in the distance is the West Coast Main Line from Carlisle station. Photograph by Bill Reed.

Above CARLISLE BOG JUNCTION

View east at Bog Junction, Carlisle, as Stanier Class 5 no. 44825 passes with an unfitted freight service. The Maryport & Carlisle Railway line joined the Newcastle & Carlisle line at this point and the curve in the distance gave access to Rome Street Goods station. Photograph by Bill Reed.

Below CARLISLE UPPERBY SHED

Stanier Class 5 no. 45070 rests in the yard at Carlisle Upperby shed during the late 1950s. The engine has the depot's '12B' shedcode, which was in use from February 1958 to December 1966, on the smokebox door and resided there from October 1957 to January 1960. Photograph by Bill Reed.

Above CARNFORTH STATION
'Britannia' no. 70014 *Iron Duke* heads north through Carnforth station with a parcels train during 1967. Photograph by Les Flint courtesy John Law.

Opposite page CARLISLE UPPERBY SHED
Stanier 'Coronation' Class Pacific no. 46238 *City of Carlisle* is at Carlisle Upperby shed on standby duty and awaits a call to action. The roundhouse is on the right and the shed offices are in the background. Photograph by Bill Reed.

Below CARNFORTH STATION
Leeds Holbeck shed's Stanier 'Jubilee' Class 4-6-0 no. 45562 *Alberta* pauses at Carnforth station with a parcels train during August 1967. Photograph by John Law.

Above CARNFORTH STATION

The first station at Carnforth was opened by the Lancaster & Carlisle Railway in September 1846. Later, other lines arrived in the town, requiring a new station and this was built in 1880. At the up main line platform in September 1967 is Class 5 no. 44872. Photograph by John Law.

Below CARNFORTH STATION

An express freight travels through Carnforth behind Class 5 no. 45000 during September 1967. The locomotive was allocated to Lostock Hall at this time and would be condemned there in October, being preserved as part of the National Collection. Photograph by John Law.

No. 45017 under the mechanical
coaler at Carnforth shed in 1968.
Photograph by Les Flint
courtesy John Law.

Above CARNFORTH SHED

View across the yard at Carnforth on 25th June 1968. The shed was only two months away from closure and a large number of locomotives are seen in the background on the scrap line; many are Stanier Class 5 4-6-0s with some Standard Class 9F 2-10-0s. Standard Class 4 4-6-0 no. 75048 is still in steam on the far right, whilst classmate no. 75009 in the foreground is stored out of service and would be scrapped at the end of the year. Fairburn Class 4P no. 42073 on the left is preserved on the Lakeside and Haverthwaite Railway. Photograph by Bill Wright.

Above CARNFORTH

A pair of Stanier Class 5s are captured at Carnforth during October 1967. No. 45424 is straight ahead with a ballast train, whilst an unidentified classmember is on the left being serviced. Picture courtesy John Law.

Opposite below CARNFORTH SHED

Over the ash pits at Carnforth shed on 28th April 1966 is Ivatt Class 4MT 2-6-0 no. 43004. The locomotive was a recent addition to the ranks at the depot and would work from Carnforth until June 1967. Photograph by Bill Wright.

Below CHESTER GENERAL STATION

A short freight train is behind Stanier 8F Class 2-8-0 no. 48090 at Chester General station on 31st January 1966. At this time the engine was at Mold Junction but would move to Chester shed in May. Photograph by Bill Wright.

Above CHESTER GENERAL STATION

Stanier 2-6-0 no. 42947 passes through Chester General station on the through lines with a holiday express running between Llandudno and Derby on 4th August 1960. Photograph by B.W.L. Brooksbank.

Below CHESTER GENERAL STATION

At the west end of Chester General Station Standard Class 9F no. 92126 is heading a down freight on 31st January 1966. The engine had 18 months left in traffic before scrapped at ten years old. Photograph by Bill Wright.

Above CHESTER DEE BRIDGE

Fowler 4F Class 0-6-0 no. 44155 of Northwich banks a freight train over the Dee Bridge (south west of Chester General) on 19th August 1963. Photograph by B.W.L. Brooksbank.

Below CHESTER GENERAL STATION

Only a month was left in traffic for Thompson B1 Class 4-6-0 no. 61166 when captured at Chester with the 11.15 ex-Llandudno to Sheffield Midland on 4th August 1962. Photograph by B.W.L. Brooksbank.

Above CHESTER GENERAL STATION

Two light engines at Chester on 1st September 1965: on the left is 9F no. 92127 and right is Class 5 no. 44913. Photograph by David Christie.

Opposite page CHESTER GENERAL STATION

Glasgow Polmadie-allocated 'Coronation Pacific no. 46230 *Duchess of Buccleuch* appears to have been a recent visitor to Crewe Works for repair and is perhaps being run in when seen at Chester. Photograph by Bill Reed.

Below CHESTER GENERAL STATION

Standard Class 4 no. 75026 and Fairburn Class 4P no. 42212 at Chester General on 24th June 1964. Photograph by David Christie.

Above CHESTER GENERAL STATION
Stanier 8F no. 48055 was constructed at the Vulcan Foundry in October 1936 and was in service until November 1967. The engine is viewed at the east end of Chester General with a mineral train on 1st September 1965. At this time no. 48055 was allocated to Mirfield. Photograph by David Christie.

Below CHESTER GENERAL STATION
Very few Stanier Class 5s were named. One of the select few was no. 45156 *Ayrshire Yeomanry*, seen here at Chester on 1st September 1965, carrying the name from 1936 until removed during the early 1960s. Subsequently, the name has been painted on the backing piece. Photograph by David Christie.

Above CHESTER GENERAL STATION

View north west from Hoole Road bridge (now Hoole Way) at the west end of Chester General to Standard Class 5MT no. 73090 which is running light engine on 24th June 1964. In the background is the ex-GWR shed. Photograph by David Christie.

Below CHESTER SHED

On Sunday, 15th May 1960, enthusiasts made a trip to Chester and stopped by the ex-LNWR depot (east of Chester General) to record the motive power resting there. In the foreground is BR Standard Class 4 4-6-0 no. 75053, allocated from October 1958 to June 1960, and right is a Stanier 2-6-0; several of the latter's other designs are visible. Photograph by Geoff Warnes.

Above CHESTER

View west from the lineside at Hoole Lane bridge, Chester (east of the station), on 22nd August 1964 as Standard Class 5 no. 73133 heads north with an express on the line to Warrington. This route was laid by the Birkenhead, Lancashire & Cheshire Junction Railway in 1850, meeting the LNWR's line south of Warrington. No. 73133 was constructed at Derby Works in September 1956 and was one of the classmembers fitted with British Caprotti valve gear in order to achieve efficiency in service and reduce maintenance costs. The engine was first allocated to Shrewsbury, then two years later moved to Patricroft depot and remained there until withdrawn in June 1968. Photograph by Bill Reed.

Opposite above CHESTER GENERAL STATION

From 1840 the Chester & Crewe Railway and the Chester & Birkenhead Railway operated separate stations in Chester. This was soon found to be disadvantageous and the two companies joined forces to open the present station which was completed in 1848 to the Italianate design of Francis Thompson. In 1970, Chester General (in use from the 1870s until 1970 to distinguish from the CLC's Chester Northgate) was given Grade II listed status and in 2005 underwent a major refurbishment project. Stanier 'Jubilee' Class 4-6-0 no. 45699 *Galatea* is running light on 22nd August 1964; the engine was condemned in November and subsequently preserved. Photograph by Bill Reed.

Opposite below CHESTER GENERAL STATION

'Britannia' Class Pacific no. 70026 *Polar Star* sweeps into Chester General from the west with an express on 22nd August 1964. Stanier Class 5 no. 45305 is at the opposite platform. Photograph by Bill Reed.

Above COPPULL

Stanier Class 5 no. 45494 heads north away from the village of Coppull (north of Wigan) with an express freight service on 13th August 1960. The train is passing Darlington's Sidings which appear to have served Coppull Ring Mill (the imposing buildings in the background) and Chisnall Hall Colliery (a short distance to the east), being named after local businessman James Darlington, who was perhaps associated with the latter. Photograph by B.W.L. Brooksbank.

Opposite above CHESTER GENERAL STATION

Stanier utilised a three-cylinder arrangement for his 2-6-4T design introduced in 1934 for use on the line to Southend. He anticipated that there would be improved acceleration by the locomotives as this was necessary to keep to the tight schedules of the services. Yet, this did not occur and when more engines of the type were required he returned to using two cylinders and 206 were erected up to 1943. No. 42482 was built as part of the second batch from Derby Works in February 1937 and was in service until April 1965. The engine has a rake of empty coaching stock at Chester on 22nd August 1964. Photograph by Bill Reed.

Opposite below CHESTER GENERAL STATION

A mixed express freight enters Chester General station behind Class 5 no. 45070 on 22nd July 1961. At this time the locomotive was allocated to Holyhead and had been there a month after leaving Crewe North, where no. 45070 had transferred from Carlisle Upperby. The engine would go on to have spells at Mold Junction, Wigan Springs Branch and Warrington Dallam depots before withdrawal in May 1967. Photograph by B.W.L. Brooksbank.

Above CREWE NORTH SHED

Posing for the camera at Crewe North during July 1964 are 'Britannia' no. 70046 *Anzac* and Type 4 (Class 40) diesel D342. Photograph by Bill Reed.

Opposite page CREWE NORTH SHED

Stanier 'Coronation' Class Pacific no. 46256 *Sir William Stanier F.R.S.* stands over the pits at Crewe North shed. Photograph by Bill Reed.

Below CREWE NORTH SHED

'Patriot' Class 4-6-0 no. 45525 *Morecambe and Heysham* had just a few months left in traffic when captured here at Crewe North in July 1964. Photograph by Bill Reed.

Above CREWE SOUTH SHED

Holbeck 8F no. 48158 appears to have been a recent visitor to Crewe Works owing to the smart appearance of the engine in place of the customary grime. Photograph by Bill Reed.

Opposite page CREWE SOUTH SHED

Willesden's 'Jubilee' Class 4-6-0 no. 45740 *Munster* visits Crewe South shed during the late 1950s before working south. Photograph by Bill Reed.

Below CREWE SOUTH SHED

This unidentifiable Ivatt Class 4MT stands outside Crewe South shed in the rain on 24th September 1967. Fifty-nine classmembers were condemned during the year followed by the final six in 1968. Photograph by Bill Reed.

Above CREWE STATION

The Manchester-Crewe section of the WCML was selected to be the first stage of electrification in 1956 and by 1960 the task was completed. Steam continued to run on the section for some time following and Fowler Class 3F 0-6-0T no. 47391 is shunting parcel vans at the north end of Crewe station on 29th September 1965. Photograph by Bill Wright.

Below CREWE STATION

Coal-weighing tender no. 10591 (built 1946) had a coal capacity of 8 tons and a 3,500-gallon water capacity and is illustrated here at Crewe Station behind no. 45298 on 25th June 1964. The pairing was the final one for the tender (of six in total) and lasted from June 1958 until September 1967. Photograph by David Christie.

Above CREWE STATION

The standard livery for Stanier's Class 5 4-6-0s was lined black from new, apart from during the war when plain black was applied for austerity, then again during the 1960s for similar reasons. No. 44865 has unlined black here at Crewe after a works visit on 23rd December 1965. The locomotive was Tyseley-allocated and was condemned at Crewe South in September 1967. Photograph by Bill Wright.

Below CREWE STATION

An early BR electric locomotive contrasts with Fowler Class 3F 0-6-0T no. 47482 at Crewe Station on 22nd June 1964. Photograph by David Christie.

Above **CREWE STATION**
Fowler 'Royal Scot' 4-6-0 no. 46150 *The Life Guardsman* has been reduced to working a local service from Crewe station on 6th April 1957. Allocated to Crewe North, the engine perhaps had a mechanical issue as admittance to works occurred at the end of the month for an unscheduled repair that took a month to complete. Photograph by Bill Reed.

Opposite above **CREWE STATION**
Just as the Stanier Class 5s underwent economy measures with livery at the end of steam so did the 'Jubilee' Class 4-6-0s. At Crewe station with an express, no. 45675 *Hardy* has unlined green livery and was one of several classmembers so treated. Under BR the engine was a long-term resident at Leeds Holbeck and was condemned there in June 1967. Photograph by Bill Reed.

Opposite below **CREWE STATION**
The Great Western Railway had access to Crewe from the early 1860s after the opening of the line from Market Drayton via Nantwich, later connected to Wellington. The company primarily wanted admission for freight traffic but also offered passenger services and GWR engines could often be spotted at Crewe. Here, Collett 'Hall' Class 4-6-0 no. 4986 *Aston Hall* has been captured at the station on 19th June 1957. Photograph by B.W.L Brooksbank.

Above CREWE STATION

Crewe station was opened during July 1837 by the Grand Junction Railway on the line between Birmingham and Warrington. In subsequent years the station became the centre for several junctions to Chester and Holyhead, Shrewsbury, Stafford and Manchester. As a result, Crewe station was rebuilt in 1867 and, following further increases in traffic, additions were made in the early 1900s. The changes made for the electrification have yet to appear in this view, taken on 19th June 1957, with Fowler 4P Class Compound 4-4-0 no. 40925, which is at the head of a parcels train. Crewe station has since been modernised in the 1980s and early 2010s and some of the original 1867 buildings have been granted Grade II listed status. Photograph by B.W.L. Brooksbank.

Opposite above CREWE STATION

In the litter-strewn surroundings of Crewe station, Fowler 3F 0-6-0T no. 47529 is engaged as a station pilot, shunting carriages from a through train on 22nd July 1961. The 3F was introduced by Fowler in 1924 and was based on the Midland Railway design produced by S.W. Johnson at the turn of the century. First appearing from Vulcan Foundry, the 3Fs were built almost exclusively by contractors up to 1930 when the total in service reached 422 examples. No. 45729 was erected by William Beardmore & Co. in March 1928 and survived until October 1961. The engine was a long-term resident at Camden depot from at least 1935 until November 1960 when transferred to Crewe South. Photograph by B.W.L. Brooksbank.

Opposite below CREWE STATION

Three engines wait to be engaged on services from Crewe station on 22nd July 1962. At the far end of the line is Nuneaton's Stanier 2-6-0 no. 42954, in the middle is Fowler 'Royal Scot' no. 46108 *Seaforth Highlander* of Carlisle Upperby and partially obscured is Type 4 diesel (Class 40) D267 which was also from Carlisle. Photograph by B.W.L. Brooksbank.

Above CREWE WORKS

Ivatt Class 2MT no. 41232 is under the attention of several fitters at Crewe Works. Picture courtesy John Law.

Below CREWE WORKS

A disparate group of locomotives were employed at Crewe Works for shunting duties. Here, Caledonian Railway Drummond 264 'Pug' Class 0-4-0ST no. 56027 has been taken on, working from January 1957 to October 1960. Photograph courtesy John Law.

Above **CREWE WORKS**
Stanier 'Jubilee' Class 4-6-0 no. 45591 *Udaipur* was erected by the North British Locomotive Company in December 1934 and was in traffic until October 1963. The engine has '5A' on the smokebox door which indicates the allocation to Crewe North that lasted from November 1956 until condemned. Photograph by Bill Reed.

Below **CREWE WORKS**
LNWR Ramsbottom 'Special Tank' 0-6-0ST no. CD7 (originally no. 2329) rests outside the Paint Shop at Crewe Works. Photograph by Bill Reed.

Above **CREWE WORKS**

Established in 1843 by the Grand Junction Railway in 1843, Crewe Works grew to be the principal locomotive workshops of the LNWR and the LMSR. The shops covered well over 100 acres on the north side of the line to Chester and at their height employed approx. 8,000 men. The last steam locomotive was erected there in late 1958 (Standard Class 9F no. 92250 was number 7,331) and the final repair was carried out on 'Britannia' no. 70013 *Oliver Cromwell* in early 1967. Some time before this event (in the late 1950s) 'Jubilee' Class no. 45674 *Duncan* is outside the Paint Shop which was located in the far north-east corner of the site. Photograph by Bill Reed.

Opposite page **CREWE WORKS**

In the yard outside the Erecting Shop at Crewe Works is Stanier 'Jubilee' Class 4-6-0 no. 45639 *Raleigh*. Two 'Britannia' Class Pacifics are also identified: no. 70043 *Lord Kitchener* and no. 70051 *Firth of Forth*. The 'Jubilee' Class were introduced by Stanier in 1934 for express passenger duties and possessed a wider route availability than Fowler's 'Royal Scot' 4-6-0s. The 'Jubilees' were built in large numbers over just a two-year period and, between 1934 and 1936, 191 were sent into service from Crewe, the NBLC and Derby. No. 45639 was completed at Crewe Works in December 1934 and was initially allocated to Crewe North before moving to Preston, then Millhouses in 1935. Just under a decade was spent at Kentish Town depot from October 1938 to September 1947, when Derby took the locomotive. There were loans to Trafford Park, Kentish Town, Bristol and Nottingham in the late 1940s and early 1950s before no. 45639 saw out the BR years at Leeds Holbeck and withdrawal came in September 1963. Photograph by Bill Reed.

Above CREWE WORKS
'Royal Scot' no. 46164 *The Artists' Rifleman* stands outside the Erecting Shop at Crewe Works. Photograph by Bill Reed.

Below CREWE WORKS
The Erecting Shop was located on the far west side of the Crewe Works site. 'Royal Scot' no. 46154 *The Hussar* is seen

Above CREWE WORKS

Revitalised and ready for a return to traffic is 'Royal Scot' no. 46100 *Royal Scot*. The engine was preserved after being condemned in October 1962. Photograph by Bill Reed.

Below CREWE WORKS

Ivatt Class 2MT no. 41288 has received a fresh application of BR's mixed traffic livery from the Paint Shop at Crewe. Photograph by Bill Reed.

Above ECCLES

Eccles station was opened on the Liverpool & Manchester Railway line on 17th September 1830. The station was subsequently rebuilt and this building survived until the 1970s and has since been replaced with modern facilities. Stanier Class 5 no. 44865 passes under Church Street bridge with a stopping train from Manchester Exchange to Liverpool on 24th July 1951. Photograph by B.W.L. Brooksbank.

Opposite above DEWSNAP SIDINGS

View west from Astley Street bridge, over the ex-Great Central Railway main line between Manchester and Sheffield (Woodhead route), Dukinfield, as Fowler 'Crab' Class 2-6-0 no. 42856 approaches Dewsnap Sidings with a mixed freight on 26th July 1951. The sidings appear to have been established in the early part of the 20th century on the site of sidings belonging to Astley Deep Pit which closed in 1901; Dukinfield Carriage & Wagons Works was also built at the same time on land belonging to the colliery across the line. In the background are Brookside Sidings and there is a curve connecting these, and the branch to Stalybridge, to the main line. The line passing underneath this, below the bridge on the right behind the signalbox, was the ex-LNWR route from Stockport and joined the ex-GCR Stalybridge line just to the north. Photograph by B.W.L. Brooksbank.

Opposite below CREWE WORKS

The Lancashire & Yorkshire Railway's Class 27 0-6-0 was designed by John Aspinall in 1889 and produced in large numbers through to 1918 when the class numbered 484. No. 52441 was erected at Horwich Works in July 1906 and would have been utilised on the company's goods trains, later for the LMSR. There was still a large number in service at Grouping, but this figure had dropped by Nationalisation and no. 52441 was one of over 200 inherited by BR. The engine was employed at Crewe Works as a shunter from April 1953 until withdrawn in September 1962 and is at the works during August 1958. Photograph by B.W.L. Brooksbank.

Opposite page EDGE LANE JUNCTION
Still in service, yet looking decidedly the worse for wear, at Edge Lane Junction on 29th February 1968 is Stanier 8F no. 48012. The engine was an early example, dating from December 1936, but was condemned in March 1968. Photograph by David Christie.

Left EDGE LANE JUNCTION
Edge Lane Junction provided a connection between the Liverpool-Manchester line at Edge Hill, Liverpool, to the Canada Dock and Bootle branch. Heading south to Edge Hill on 29th February 1968 is 8F no. 48746. Photograph by David Christie.

Below EDGE HILL, LIVERPOOL
Stanier 8F no. 48723 is viewed next to Engine Shed Junction signal box, Edge Hill, Liverpool, on 29th February 1968. Photograph by David Christie.

Above FARINGTON JUNCTION
A distance to the north of the village of Farington (south of Preston) the L&YR line from Liverpool to Blackburn crossed over the WCML. Farington Junction box (seen here) oversaw the south/east fork and the exchange sidings on the right. Stanier Class 5 no. 44894 has also been captured light engine on 24th June 1968. Photograph by Bill Wright.

Below EDGE HILL, LIVERPOOL
'Jubilee' no. 45703 *Thunderer* approaches Edge Hill station with the 09.15 express from Birmingham New Street to Lime Street on 12th June 1959. Photograph by B.W.L. Brooksbank.

Above FARINGTON STATION
View from Fowler Lane bridge as 9F no. 92016 passes Farington Junction with a freight train on 18th September 1965. Photograph by B.W.L. Brooksbank.

Below FARINGTON
Class 5 no. 45195 pilots 'Patriot' Class 45537 *Private E. Sykes, V.C.* through Farington station with the 07.30 Aberdeen to Manchester Victoria express on 1st August 1959. Photograph by B.W.L. Brooksbank.

Above FARINGTON STATION
An up freight travels through Farington station behind Hughes 'Crab' no. 42841 on 20th June 1957. Photograph by B.W.L. Brooksbank.

Below FRODSHAM STATION
View south from the footbridge over the Birkenhead Railway's Chester-Warrington line at Frodsham station on 22nd August 1964. Heading the 16.20 Holyhead to Manchester express is Stanier Class 5 no. 45132. Photograph by B.W.L. Brooksbank.

Above GARSTANG

Leading a freight train southward near Garstang (between Lancaster and Preston) in mid-1967 is Stanier Class 5 no. 44817. Picture courtesy John Law.

Below FLEETWOOD

Johnson 3F Class 0-6-0 no. 43502 has been left to rust at Fleetwood on 18th September 1960. The engine was condemned at the depot in December 1959 but would not go for scrap until 1962. Photograph by Geoff Warnes.

Above GODLEY JUNCTION
Robinson 9K (LNER C13) Class 4-4-2T no. 67437 travels east with a local service away from Godley Junction station on the ex-GCR Manchester to Sheffield 'Woodhead' route on 28th July 1951. The locomotive was one of forty locomotives erected by the Vulcan Foundry and Gorton Works to the design, emerging from the latter in May 1905 as no. 114. At Nationalisation the engine was allocated to Gorton shed and was withdrawn from there in August 1957. Photograph by B.W.L. Brooksbank.

Opposite above GODLEY JUNCTION
Approaching Godley Junction with an express from Cleethorpes to Manchester on 28th July 1951 is Thompson B1 Class 4-6-0 no. 61160. A scheme to electrify the line from Sheffield to Manchester was instigated by the LNER in the late 1930s and was progressing with the installation of the overhead gantries when war was declared. The project restarted after the war but was delayed by the need for a new tunnel under the Pennines. Completed in the mid-1950s, the line was only open for passenger services until 1970 and freight ceased in 1981, with the track east of Hadfield latterly being lifted. Photograph by B.W.L. Brooksbank.

Opposite below GLAZEBROOK
War Department 'Austerity' Class 2-8-0 no. 90278 travels steadily westward towards Warrington on the Cheshire Line Committee's Manchester-Liverpool line. The engine has just passed through Glazebrook station with a freight train on 21st June 1957. Photograph by B.W.L. Brooksbank.

Above **GORTON WORKS**

On the scrap line at Gorton Works — with most of the work having been undertaken — in March 1963 is J11 Class no. 64354. Picture courtesy Rail Photoprints.

Opposite above **GORTON WORKS**

Robinson J11 0-6-0 no. 64373 under repair in the Erecting Shop at Gorton Works. The Manchester, Sheffield & Lincolnshire Railway (later GCR) established the shops on the north side of the main line at Gorton in 1848, primarily for repairs at first, later undertaking construction of new engines from 1857. The works were upgraded and expanded regularly throughout the late 19th century, but the choice of site was poor and eventually the Carriage & Wagon Department was transferred to Dukinfield in the early 20th century. Under the LNER, Gorton mainly focussed on repairs, although some new construction was carried out up to the late 1930s. After Nationalisation the workshops were solely used for repairs and in the 1950s took on the electric locomotives used for the Woodhead line. BR had to close several shops in the early 1960s and Gorton was a victim in 1963 with the loss of 1,500 jobs. Picture courtesy Rail Photoprints.

Opposite below **GORTON WORKS**

Under LNER Chief Mechanical Engineer Edward Thompson, Gorton Works was involved with several schemes that saw locomotives rebuilt in a bid to achieve greater efficiency and standardisation. An example of this occurred to a number of Robinson's 8K (LNER O4) Class 2-8-0s in the 1940s and saw the B1-type boiler, cylinders and motion fitted; the engines were then classified O1. No. 63678 (built at Gorton in May 1912) was modified in December 1944 and subsequently became one of a number of O1s used at Annesley shed for the express freight services to Woodford Halse on the ex-GCR main line. The engine is in Gorton Works' yard after a repair in 1948. Picture from the Malcolm Crawley Collection.

Above HARTFORD JUNCTION

Hodge Lane bridge, north west of Hartford, provides the vantage point for the two images on this page. Here, a coal train has left the WCML and takes the Hertford Loop to join the CLC's Chester-Northwich line; the engine is Class 5 no. 45071 on 12th April 1966. Photograph by B.W.L. Brooksbank.

Below HARTFORD JUNCTION

Stanier 8F no. 48693 heads towards the WCML with a limestone train from Tunstead to ICI Winnington on 30th June 1964. Photograph by B.W.L. Brooksbank.

Above HEATON MERSEY SHED

Two of Stanier's 2-6-0s are outside the shed at Heaton Mersey on 8th August 1965. On the left is no. 42967 and right is no. 42955. Both engines were erected at Crewe Works between December 1933 and January 1934, later arriving at Heaton Mersey together in May 1965. Photograph by Bill Wright.

Below HEATON MERSEY SHED

Another of Heaton Mersey's Stanier 2-6-0s — no. 42947 — is captured outside the shed, this time with 9F no. 92054 for company on 8th August 1965. Photograph by Bill Wright.

HEATON MERSEY SHED

Situated on the south side of the CLC's line between Stockport-Altrincham and near the junction between this route and the ex-Midland Railway Manchester South District Line (Manchester Central-Stockport), Heaton Mersey shed was built by the CLC in the late 1880s. The building had eight roads and a coal stage and turntable (50 ft) were also provided. All eight roads are occupied here on 8th August 1965, including four Stanier 2-6-0s. Photograph by Bill Wright.

HEATON MERSEY SHED
Heaton Mersey depot received a new 70 ft turntable in the early 1950s as part of a BR improvement scheme. Stanier 8F no. 48191 is on the apparatus during early 1968; the shed was closed in May. Photograph by Bill Reed.

HEST BANK STATION

Fowler 4P Class 2-6-4T is seen at Hest Bank station with the 17.23 service from Windermere to Liverpool during September 1963. Photograph by Bill Reed.

Above HEST BANK STATION

An unidentified 'Jubilee' Class 4-6-0 rushes through Hest Bank station on 19th September 1964. On the right, camping coaches can be observed in the station's goods yard which closed at the end of 1963. Photograph by Geoff Warnes.

Below HEST BANK STATION

Opened by the Lancaster & Carlisle Railway on 22nd September 1846, Hest Bank station served the local area until 3rd February 1969 when closed by BR. Two Stanier Class 5s are at the station on 19th August 1967. Photograph courtesy John Law.

Above HEST BANK STATION
Stanier Class 5 no. 45424 approaches Hest Bank with an up express on 19th August 1967. Photograph by Les Flint courtesy John Law.

Below HORWICH WORKS
Two withdrawn ex-Lancashire & Yorkshire Railway locomotives stand in the yard at Horwich Works on 15th May 1960. Aspinall 27 Class 0-6-0 no. 52268 and 23 Class 0-6-0ST no. 51457 were not broken up on site but diverted to private scrap yards. Photograph by Geoff Warnes.

Above **HOOTON STATION**

BR 9F no. 92163 is held at Hooton station with an up empty mineral train on 16th September 1965. A diesel railcar is passing by on the right. Photograph by B.W.L. Brooksbank.

Below **HOOTON STATION**

Fowler 3F 0-6-0T no. 47627 makes a light engine movement through Hooton station on 16th September 1965. Photograph by B.W.L. Brooksbank.

Above LANCASTER CASTLE STATION
Stanier Class 5 no. 45390 waits to be released from a stop signal on the down fast line at Lancaster station on 5th August 1967. Photograph by Bill Wright.

Opposite above KIRKHAM & WESHAM STATION
Heavy traffic for the Blackpool illuminations has forced WD 'Austerity' no. 90645 into action on an empty stock working on 8th September 1962. The locomotive has been captured from Station Road bridge (looking west) to Kirkham Junction where the Lytham line diverged from the route to Blackpool Central. Photograph by B.W.L. Brooksbank.

Opposite below KIRKHAM & WESHAM STATION
Stanier 'Jubilee' Class no. 45575 *Madras* speeds through Kirkham & Wesham station with an 'Illuminations Special' from Burton-on-Trent/Derby on 8th September 1962. Photograph by B.W.L. Brooksbank.

Above LANCASTER CASTLE STATION

Sweeping into Lancaster station on 5th August 1967 is Stanier Class 5 no. 44911 which is at the head of the southbound 11.05 Glasgow to Blackpool express. The locomotive was based at several sheds under BR and interestingly had a spell at King's Cross depot from February 1956 until May 1957. Photograph by Bill Wright.

Below LANCASTER CASTLE STATION

No. 45321 approaches Lancaster Castle station with an up freight on 5th August 1967. Photograph by Bill Wright.

Above LANCASTER

A short distance south of Lancaster, 'Britannia' Class Pacific no. 70010 *Owen Glendower* rushes along with an up express from Barrow on 26th August 1967. Photograph by David Christie.

Below LANCASTER GREEN AYRE STATION

The crew of an unidentified Class 5 takes to the footplate before departing with an express from Lancaster to Leeds on 19th September 1964. Photograph by Geoff Warnes.

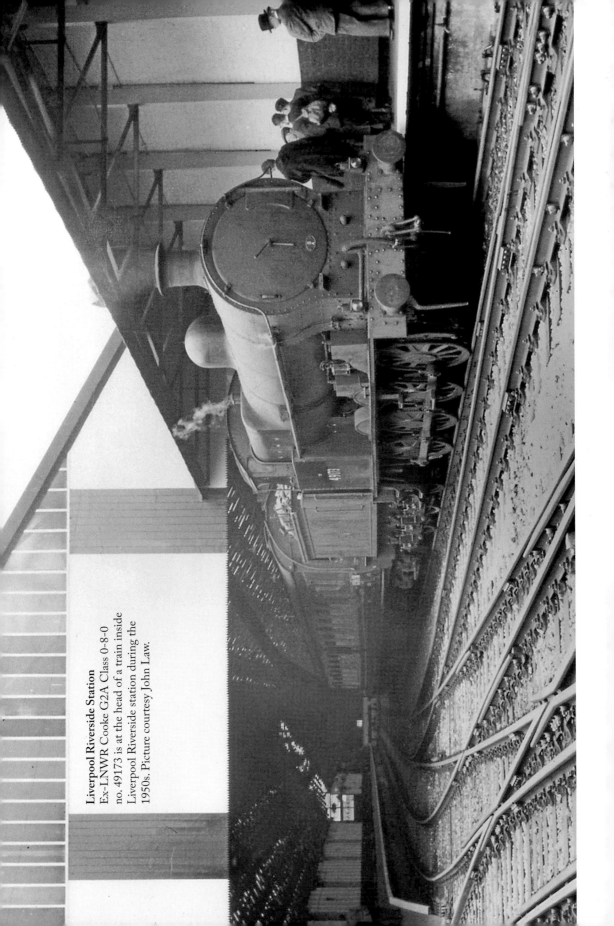

Liverpool Riverside Station
Ex-LNWR Cooke G2A Class 0-8-0 no. 49173 is at the head of a train inside Liverpool Riverside station during the 1950s. Picture courtesy John Law.

Above LIVERPOOL LIME STREET STATION

Fowler 'Patriot' no. 45515 *Caernarvon* is at platform six with the 10.05 express from Liverpool Lime Street to Bournemouth West, 13th June 1959. Photograph by B.W.L. Brooksbank.

Below LIVERPOOL LIME STREET STATION

On 10th June 1959, 'Jubilee' no. 45670 *Howard of Effingham* (left) stands at the head of the 10.05 express from Lime Street to Birmingham and a Stanier 4P Class 2-6-4T (right) reversing out after working a service from Wigan via St Helens. Photograph by B.W.L. Brooksbank.

Above and Below LIVERPOOL LIME STREET STATION

Two views, taken on 24th June 1964, at Liverpool Lime Street station. Fowler Class 3F 0-6-0T no. 47485 and Fairburn 4P Class 2-6-4T no. 42132 are seen, first reversing on to a train, then taking the service out from the platform. No. 47485 was erected at Vulcan Foundry in January 1928 as part of Lot 50 which saw a total of 49 completed at the works. The engine mainly worked in the Midlands under BR and moved to Edge Hill in November 1963, being condemned there in January 1965. No. 42132 was a good deal younger than no. 47485, having been constructed at Derby in December 1949 and initially worked from St Albans before transferring northward. No. 42132 was employed at Southport from July 1961 to June 1966 and withdrawal occurred soon after. Both pictures by David Christie.

Above and Below **LIVERPOOL, SEFTON PARK**

On the line from Speke to Edge Hill, Sefton Park station was closed during May 1960 due to low passenger numbers. Around this time the site has been used to provide the vantage point for these two images. Above, Class 5 no. 44864 is leading a freight train and below, classmate no. 45446 charges towards Liverpool Lime Street with an express from Crewe. Both photographs by Rev. J. David Benson courtesy A1 Steam Trust.

Above **LOSTOCK HALL STATION**
The East Lancashire Railway opened Lostock Hall station (south of Preston, not to be confused with Lostock station west of Bolton) on 2nd April 1849 as a modest facility to serve the local area. Later, closure of the station occurred on 6th October 1969, although the line was saved due to local opposition. Following further campaigning, the station was restored on 14th May 1984 and is still open. During 1964, Fowler 3F 0-6-0T no. 47293 passes through the station with a freight train. Photograph by John Arnott-Brown courtesy A1 Steam Trust.

Opposite above **LIVERPOOL NEWSHAM PARK**
Travelling tender-first on the Canada Dock and Bootle branch at Newsham Park, Liverpool, on 29th February 1968 is Stanier 8F no. 48692. The engine, which is about to pass under Lister Road bridge with a freight train, has '8A' chalked on the smokebox door, leaving no doubt the engine was employed at Edge Hill depot, occupying the period September 1967 to May 1968. No. 48692 would move to Bolton but was condemned there in June 1968. Photograph by David Christie.

Opposite below **LIVERPOOL LIME STREET STATION**
View east towards the tunnels at Liverpool Lime Street station on 10th June 1959. On the left Stanier 4P Class 2-6-4T no. 42607 has charge of a local service, whilst an express gets away on the right. Both engines faced a stiff climb on exiting the station, with gradients of 1 in 83, 1 in 93 and 1 in 136 for the 1½ miles out to Edge Hill. This was quite a challenge for locomotives in the early years of the railways and these were removed and attached at Edge Hill. The train either descended into the station with brake vehicles connected or was hauled out using a stationary steam engine and ropes. This practice, which was not uncommon, carried on until the 1870s. Photograph by B.W.L. Brooksbank.

Opposite page and above LOSTOCK HALL SHED

Two images captured near the end of steam, 4th August 1968. 'Britannia' Class Pacific no. 70013 *Oliver Cromwell* is featured in both instances, along with Stanier 8F no. 48493, at Lostock Hall shed. No. 70013 was taking a break from working railtours, having two scheduled on this day. The first saw the engine travelling from Manchester to Blackburn and the second took *Oliver Cromwell* from Lostock Hall to Manchester and Stockport. Both pictures by David Christie.

LOSTOCK HALL SHED

Stanier 8F no. 48723 stands in the shed yard at Lostock Hall on 24th June 1968. Photograph by Bill Wright.

Above **LOSTOCK HALL SHED**

Lostock Hall shed was an eight-road building of major importance for traffic in the local area. In the shed yard on 28th April 1966 are Stanier Class 5 no. 44819 and Stanier 8F no. 48470. Photograph by Bill Wright.

Below **LOSTOCK HALL SIDINGS**

Lostock Hall goods sidings were just east of Lostock Hall station on the north side of the ex-L&YR line from Liverpool to Blackburn and connected to the WCML via the Farington Fork. Stanier 8F no. 48423 appears to be pulling a train out of the goods sidings and heading west on 28th April 1966. Photograph by Bill Wright.

Above MANCHESTER EXCHANGE STATION
Arriving at platform 3 with an unidentified express on 3rd September 1960 is Stanier 'Jubilee' Class no. 45738 *Samson*. On the left Standard Class 5 no. 73163 heads the 15.15 to Huddersfield and Bradford. Photograph by B.W.L. Brooksbank.

Below MANCHESTER LONDON ROAD STATION
Robinson J11 0-6-0 no. 4401 poses at Manchester London Road station on 19th June 1948. The engine was renumbered 64401 over a year later. Photograph by B.W.L. Brooksbank.

Above MANCHESTER VICTORIA STATION

Miles Platting bank lay in wait for trains travelling north west out of Manchester Victoria station. The acclivity had gradients of 1 in 59 and 1 in 47 for approx. 1.5 miles and accordingly bankers were provided. Fairburn 4MT no. 42087 is waiting to be called into action on 27th July 1966. Photograph by B.W.L. Brooksbank.

Below MANCHESTER VICTORIA STATION

Stanier 8F no. 48263 passes through Manchester Victoria with a local freight service on 27th July 1966. Photograph by B.W.L. Brooksbank.

MANCHESTER VICTORIA STATION

Stanier 8F no. 48111 leads a mineral train
through Manchester Victoria on 10th July 1967.
Photograph by Bill Wright.

Above MANCHESTER VICTORIA STATION
Stanier Class 5 no. 45255 (and footplateman) waits for a train that requires banking assistance from Manchester Victoria on 14th June 1968. Photograph by Bill Wright.

Below MANCHESTER PICCADILLY STATION
Rebuilding work at Manchester London Road station, which became Piccadilly, on 11th April 1960. Photograph by B.W.L. Brooksbank.

Above MANCHESTER VICTORIA STATION

Newton Heath-allocated Class 5 no. 44910 is at Manchester Victoria on 2nd March 1968; the engine was condemned in June. Photograph by David Christie.

Below MANCHESTER VICTORIA STATION

Relatively immaculate Class 5 no. 45156 *Ayrshire Yeomanry* is seen with a parcels train on 14th June 1968. Photograph by Bill Wright.

Above MANCHESTER VICTORIA STATION
The fireman of 8F no. 48652 takes a break as the train passes through Manchester Victoria station on 14th June 1968. Photograph by Bill Wright.

Below MANCHESTER VICTORIA EAST JUNCTION
Standard Class 5 no. 73004 transports a mixed freight past Manchester Victoria East Junction signal box on 10th July 1967. The box was specially built in 1962 and replaced several smaller ones in the area. Photograph by Bill Wright.

Above MANCHESTER VICTORIA STATION

Only a small number of Stanier 8Fs were erected at Ashford Works to REC orders during the war. No. 48620 was one of just fourteen completed there and entered traffic during November 1943. The engine is travelling towards Manchester Victoria station with a long train of mineral wagons on 10th July 1967; withdrawal occurred in June 1968. Photograph by Bill Wright.

Above MANCHESTER VICTORIA STATION
Stopped by a signal at Manchester Victoria station, Standard Class 5 no. 73142 waits patiently to be released and continue with an engineer's train on 10th July 1967. The locomotive was one of 30 classmembers fitted with British Caprotti valve gear and poppet valves. Photograph by Bill Wright.

Below MANCHESTER VICTORIA STATION
Just three months in service remained for Class 5 no. 44938 when at Manchester Victoria on 10th July 1967. Photograph by Bill Wright.

Above MANCHESTER VICTORIA STATION
Stanier Class 5 no. 45255 is on banking duty, 14th June 1968. Photograph by Bill Wright.

Below MANCHESTER VICTORIA STATION
Another view of no. 73142 with an engineer's train on 10th July 1967. Allocated to Patricroft depot at this time (from June 1964), the locomotive was condemned at the shed in April 1968. Photograph by Bill Wright.

Above MANCHESTER CENTRAL STATION
Robinson D10 Class 4-4-0 no. 62656 *Sir Clement Royds* is on Manchester Central station's turntable during the early 1950s. Photograph by Geoff Warnes.

Below MARPLE VIADUCT
Robinson C14 Class 4-4-2T no. 67447 crosses Marple Viaduct with a local service in the early 1950s. Photograph by Geoff Warnes.

Above NEWTON HEATH SHED

Stanier 8F no. 48678 stands in the shed yard at Newton Heath with classmate no. 48356. Both engines were constructed in June 1944, but at different workshops; no. 48678 was the product of Brighton, while no. 48356 was completed at Horwich. The two locomotives were amongst a number of 8Fs that were built with features that differed from the original specifications for the class. Problems were arising from the thickness of the frames being too thin and in May 1944 the width was increased to 1 ⅛ in. from 1 ⁵⁄₁₆ in. used previously. Material shortages at the time also caused the adoption of integrally cast balance weights on the wheels instead of the built-up type used hitherto. No. 48678 and no. 48356 were late arrivals to Newton Heath shed (December 1967 and May 1968 respectively) and were condemned there in June 1968. Photograph by Bill Reed.

Opposite page MORECAMBE PROMENADE STATION

Morecambe Northumberland Road station originally served the town and resort of Morecambe from mid-1848 and was opened on the 'Little' North Western Railway line between Skipton-Lancaster-Morecambe. The Midland Railway took over the company not long afterwards and in the early 20th century decided that Northumberland Road was not meeting the traffic requirements and a new station — Morecambe Promenade — was completed by early 1907. This was much larger than the predecessor as the company expected high levels of holiday traffic. During the following year the line to Heysham was electrified and overhead gantries were installed (seen here) and remained in use until the early 1960s. Pictured at the station with a local service during July 1964 is Stanier 'Jubilee' Class no. 45573 *Newfoundland*. The engine was a long-term resident at Leeds Holbeck shed and was withdrawn from there in September 1965. Photograph by Bill Reed.

Above MUSPRATT'S SIDINGS

Just west of Flint station on the Chester to Holyhead line, Stanier Class 5 no. 45344 is travelling westward past Muspratt's Sidings with the 08.25 Coventry to Llandudno on 29th August 1964. The sidings were connected to the extensive chemical works in the area once operated by Muspratt Bros & Huntly. The locomotive was built by Armstrong Whitworth in April 1937 and was in service until August 1966. At the time of the image the engine was allocated to Crewe North, but moved on to Chester at the end of the year and from there was transferred to Croes Newydd in October 1965. Photograph by B.W.L. Brooksbank.

Opposite above NEWTON HEATH SHED

Stored and rusting away amidst wildflowers at Newton Heath shed is Fowler 4F Class 0-6-0 no. 44247. The locomotive — seen on 8th August 1965 — was close to withdrawal (December) and likely did not re-enter service. Interestingly, the engine possesses a cab weatherboard, signifying that at one time (perhaps the winter of 1964/1965) a snow plough was fitted, which is further evidenced by the lack of buffers and bufferbeam where the apparatus would have been attached. No. 44247 is noted in *LMS Locomotive Profiles No. 10 — The Standard Class 4 Goods 0-6-0s* as having been a snow plough in the late 1950s when allocated to Peterborough Spital Bridge shed. Photograph by Bill Wright.

Opposite below NEWTON HEATH SHED

Newton Heath depot was a very large facility erected by the Lancashire & Yorkshire Railway in 1876, possessing 24 roads under cover. The shed was located just west of Newton Heath station (closed 1966) between the Manchester-Oldham line and Manchester-Rochdale route. Under BR, part of the depot was turned over to DMUs in the late 1950s (one can be seen on the right, along with the new building) and later diesel locomotives; this is a role the site continues to hold today. Back in August 1964 the shed was still very much concerned with steam and two Stanier 4-6-0s are in the yard being serviced. On the left is 'Jubilee' no. 45592 *Indore* and to the right is Class 5 no. 45381. The aforementioned would be withdrawn at the end of the following month, whilst the latter survived until May 1968. Photograph by Bill Reed.

Above NEWTON HEATH SHED

Despite lacking a shedplate, Stanier Class 5 no. 45025 is identified as belonging to Carnforth shed through the information being scrawled on the bufferbeam, in addition to previously being written on the top half of the smokebox. The engine has worked south from there to Manchester and is being serviced at Newton Heath on 2nd March 1968. Withdrawn at the end of steam, no. 45025 was subsequently preserved and based at the Strathspey Railway; the locomotive is currently undergoing an overhaul. Photograph by David Christie.

Above NORTHWICH

Two Robinson O4 2-8-0s are seen at Northwich on 15th May 1960. No. 63700 (right) had just six months left in traffic and no. 63649 had nine remaining; both were condemned at Gorton. Photograph by Geoff Warnes.

Below NORTHWICH SHED

An unidentified O4 and two Robinson D11 'Director' Class 4-4-0s stand around the turntable at Northwich shed on 23rd March 1956. The depot was operated by the CLC, then LNER before Nationalisation when absorbed by the London Midland Region. Photograph by Geoff Warnes.

Above and Below NORTHWICH SHED
Being a small depot, Northwich had to carry out running repairs using a pair of shear legs located in the yard. D11 no. 62665 *Mons* creates a dramatic sight for enthusiasts on 23rd March 1956. Photograph by Geoff Warnes.

Above NORTHWICH SHED

A small group of D11 'Director' Class 4-4-0s were based at Northwich during the mid-1950s, one being no. 62669 *Ypres* which stands to the west of the shed near the station (in the background). Photograph by Geoff Warnes.

Below ORMSKIRK STATION

View north from Derby Street road bridge to Ormskirk station in 1964 as BR Standard Class 4 no. 75046 stops at the station with a southbound local service. Photograph by John Arnott-Brown courtesy A1 Steam Trust.

Above PATRICROFT SHED

A locomotive shed was established at Patricroft by the LNWR in 1885 and the building possessed eight roads that entered from the south west. A second building was constructed by the company in 1904 and this increased the number of lines under cover by ten. The first shed stands here behind Fowler 4P Class 2-6-4T no. 42343 on 8th August 1965. By this time the number of lines had been reduced to four and a new roof had been installed by BR. Both sheds closed to steam in July 1968 and later demolished, the site being occupied by industrial units and bounded by the M602 motorway. Photograph by Bill Wright.

Opposite above PATRICROFT SHED

Stanier 8F no. 48321 was one of thirty locomotives erected at Crewe Works between September 1943 and May 1944 to Lot No. 159. No. 48321 has subsequently seen alterations from new at the front end through the addition of Automatic Warning System (AWS) apparatus and the lowering of the top lamp iron due to concerns of electric shock from overhead wires; the centre lamp iron has also been moved to the right. Having lost the shedplate, '9D' has been painted on to the smokebox door, denoting an allocation to Newton Heath which lasted from July 1964 until the engine's withdrawal in June 1968. No. 48321 is at Patricroft (new) shed on 1st March 1968. Photograph by David Christie.

Opposite below PATRICROFT SHED

Patricroft shed was located in the midst of a complex set of railway lines between Eccles and Patricroft stations on the Liverpool & Manchester Railway. The latter bounded the site on the southern side, whilst to the north east were Patricroft Sidings and the Manchester-Wigan-Bolton route. To the north west was the Clifton Branch (connecting with the Manchester to Bury line) and more sidings belonging to the engineering works of Mitchell, Shackleton & Co. The site is depicted on 1st March 1968 from a footbridge over the main line, with two BR Standard Class Fives featuring; no. 73067 and 73125. Photograph by David Christie.

Above PRESTON STATION

At the north end of Preston station on 26th June 1964 are two Stanier Class 5s. Nearest is no. 45101, which was erected at the Vulcan Foundry during May 1935, and just getting away is no. 44697. The latter was a relative youngster, having been built at Horwich in November 1950 and was amongst the final classmembers completed. The engine was part of a group of 28 constructed at Horwich and these were fitted with Timken roller bearings on the driving axle as part of experiments conducted to increase mileages between repairs. No. 44697 was later the recipient of a coal-weighing tender and this was carried from January 1951 until withdrawal in November 1967. The locomotive was allocated to Newton Heath shed at this time and had been from September 1953; no. 45101 was also based there when condemned in March 1968, first arriving in September 1956. Photograph by David Christie.

Opposite page PATRICROFT SHED

Stanier 8F no. 48714 was one of the classmembers built for the LNER at Brighton Works during the war, entering traffic in July 1944. The locomotive was numbered 7660 in the LNER stock book and subsequently carried no. 3109 as part of CME Edward Thompson's renumbering scheme of 1946. With the arrival of WD 'Austerity' 2-8-0s on the LNER, the 8Fs (LNER Class O6) were renumbered and the engine became no. 3509 before being repatriated to the LMSR in November 1947, taking no. 8714. The engine was at Rose Grove shed for Nationalisation and had spells at several others in the area before arriving at Patricroft in May 1963. Agecroft depot took no. 48714 for a spell between January and October 1966 before a return was made to Patricroft. Captured in the new shed's yard on 8th August 1965, the locomotive still carries Wakefield mechanical lubricators (placed almost centrally on the footplate between the two sandboxes) which were standard on the LNER and fitted to the 25 Brighton engines in place of the LMSR's favoured Silvertown type. Photograph by Bill Wright.

Above and Below PRESTON STATION

Two images of Stanier Class 5 no. 45017 as the engine arrives at Preston station with a short parcels train on 30th June 1967. Working from Carnforth shed at this time, the locomotive was withdrawn from there at the end of steam. Photograph by Bill Wright.

Above **PRESTON STATION**

The 13.27 Manchester to Glasgow express waits behind impatient Stanier Class 5 no. 45187 at Preston station on 30th June 1967. The engine was allocated to Edge Hill depot and had been from the start of the decade. Moving to Patricroft in May 1968, withdrawal occurred a month later. Photograph by Bill Wright.

PRESTON STATION
Stanier Class 5 no. 44971 has relieved Class 47 D1752 of the 11.30 Glasgow to Manchester express on 30th June 1967. Photograph by Bill Wright.

PRESTON STATION

Stanier 8F no. 48493 passes under Fishergate bridge, Preston, with the 10.40 Burnley to Burn Naze coal train on 24th June 1968. Photograph by Bill Wright.

Above PRESTON STATION

Stanier 'Coronation' Pacific no. 46250 *City of Lichfield* is seen at Preston station with an express on 28th October 1962. The engine was a long-term resident of Carlisle Upperby shed (June 1958 to September 1964 when withdrawn). Photograph by Bill Reed.

Opposite above PRESTON STATION

A pair of Gresley K3 Class 2-6-0s has strayed far from home territory with this relief express from Blackpool on 13th August 1960. No. 61853 is piloting no. 61975 and both engines had travelled from Leeds with the train, which was returning via Blackburn, Burnley and Sowerby Bridge for Leeds Central station. The locomotives were allocated to Ardsley depot at this time and both moved to Low Moor, Bradford, in June 1961. No. 61975 was condemned there in September, yet no. 61853 — some 11 years older (March 1925) — returned to Ardsley and was not withdrawn until December 1962. Photograph by B.W.L. Brooksbank.

Opposite below PRESTON STATION

View south from the footbridge connecting the platforms at Preston station on 23rd July 1966. Working on station pilot duties at platform six is Fairburn 4P Class 2-6-4T no. 42105. The locomotive was built at Brighton Works in September 1950 and was in traffic until November 1966. Initially allocated to Tunbridge Wells shed, the engine remained with the Southern Region until 1959 and then had spells at Bletchley, Willesden and Carnforth before the final move was made to Lostock Hall in October 1965. Photograph by B.W.L. Brooksbank.

Above SALFORD STATION

An empty stock train headed by BR Standard Class 4 4-6-0 no. 75015 travels eastward through Salford station to Manchester Victoria on 9th June 1959. In the background is the station's signalbox which was located at the end of platforms 3/4. The box has since been removed and the platforms have also been taken out of use. Photograph by B.W.L. Brooksbank.

Opposite above ROCHDALE STATION

Dating from November 1896, ex-L&YR Aspinall Class 27 0-6-0 no. 52343 was still hard at work nearly 55 years later. The locomotive is at Rochdale station on 24th April 1950, perhaps shunting this van, and would continue in service until August 1956. Allocated to Low Moor depot at this time, no. 52343 had been there from 1953 and had previously resided at Newton Heath from at least Nationalisation. Photograph by B.W.L. Brooksbank.

Opposite below ROCHDALE STATION

Stanier Class 5 no. 45375 is seen light engine just to the east of Rochdale station on 8th July 1961. The station was opened by the Manchester & Leeds Railway in 1839 and subsequently rebuilt by the Lancashire & Yorkshire Railway in the late 1880s. The new station possessed eight platforms, but from the 1970s this number has been reduced due to the decline to local services. Photograph by B.W.L. Brooksbank.

Above SALFORD STATION

Thompson O4/7 Class 2-8-0 no. 63794 is passing through Salford station whilst making an unusual freight transfer on 18th April 1962. The engine is at the head of a mixed cattle/van/wagon train from Dewsnap Sidings to Trafford Park. Photograph by B.W.L. Brooksbank.

Below SALFORD STATION

The 16.30 express from Manchester Exchange to Llandudno has Stanier Class 5s no. 45316 and no. 44780 leading the way through Salford station on 24th August 1963. Photograph by B.W.L. Brooksbank.

Above SALFORD STATION

Stanier 'Jubilee' Class 4-6-0 no. 45650 *Blake* is at Salford with the 15.54 Manchester Exchange to Barrow-in-Furness express on 9th June 1959. Photograph by B.W.L. Brooksbank.

Below SALFORD STATION

A train of empty stock is hauled away from Manchester Exchange station by Hughes 'Crab' 2-6-0 no. 42810 on 24th August 1963. Photograph by B.W.L. Brooksbank.

Above SALWICK STATION

View west from Salwick station as Stanier Class 5 no. 45190 passes through with a Blackpool-Bletchley relief express on 1st August 1959. Photograph by B.W.L. Brooksbank.

Below SALWICK STATION

Ex-LNER stock forms the 13.05 train from Blackpool to West Hartlepool on 1st August 1959. Hughes 'Crab' Class no. 42717 of Rose Grove shed leads the 'foreign' carriages. Photograph by B.W.L. Brooksbank.

Above SCOUT GREEN

Two Stanier Class 5s climb the 1 in 75 at Scout Green between Tebay and Shap on the WCML. Viewed on 23rd June 1967, no. 45227 is piloting whilst the train engine is 44682. Photograph by David Christie.

Below SCOUT GREEN

After working hard up Shap incline as a banker, BR Standard Class 4 no. 75032 glides back down to Tebay to wait for the next duty. Photograph by David Christie.

SCOUT GREEN
With assistance from the rear, Stanier
Class 5 no. 44852 climbs past Scout
Green with a down freight on 23rd June
1967. Photograph by David Christie.

SCOUT GREEN
Another view of Stanier Class 5s no. 45227 and 44682 tackling Shap bank on 23rd June 1967. At this time the locomotives were allocated to Lostock Hall and Stoke respectively. Photograph by David Christie.

Above SHAP

Stanier Class 5 no. 45054 reaches Shap with a van train on 23rd June 1967. Withdrawal from Carnforth occurred in February 1968. Photograph by David Christie.

Below SHAP

The clean exhaust and fireman leaning out of the cab window confirm that Stanier Class 5 no. 45043 is travelling down Shap bank towards Tebay with this mixed goods train on 22nd June 1967. Photograph by David Christie.

SOUTHPORT
View north west from a footbridge over the lines at Southport station during August 1956. Stanier 3P Class 2-6-2T no. 40192 departs with a local train for Preston. Picture courtesy *Yorkshire Post Newspapers*.

Above SOUTHPORT STATION

View east at Southport station as Stanier Class 5 no. 44728 arrives with an express from Manchester in August 1956. Picture courtesy *Yorkshire Post Newspapers*.

Below SPRINGS BRANCH JUNCTION

Several lines met the WCML south of Wigan. Springs Branch ran there from the north east serving several industrial sites. At the junction for the line, Stanier Class 5 no. 45163 passes by heading south with the 11.00 Windermere to Crewe on 3rd May 1965. Photograph by B.W.L. Brooksbank.

Above SPEKE JUNCTION SHED
The line to Liverpool branched off from the Widnes to Garston route just west of Speke station at Speke Junction. There were a number of sidings in this area and in 1886 the LNWR opened a new 12-track shed in the midst of the junction and sidings. The shed is seen here near to closure on 29th February 1968 with Stanier Class 5 no. 45212 identifiable. Photograph by David Christie.

Below SPEKE JUNCTION SHED
Stanier Class 5 no. 45279 of Heaton Mersey visits Speke Junction depot on 29th February 1968, whilst classmate no. 45201 is on home ground. Photograph by David Christie.

Above STOCKPORT EDGELEY SHED

Servicing facilities for locomotives at Stockport were initially provided by the Stockport, Timperley & Altrincham Junction Railway near Tiviot Dale station in 1866. The LNWR did not build substantial servicing facilities until 1883 when an eight-track shed was opened on the west side of the line from Crewe on the southern approach to Stockport Edgeley station; the shed was also just north of the junction for the line to Buxton. The shed managed to survive until May 1968 and the site has since been repurposed for occupation by industrial units. A cold morning on 2nd March 1968 sees two Stanier Class 5s outside the depot. To the left is no. 45013, which was a recent addition to the ranks from Carlisle Kingmoor, and right (missing numberplate) is no. 44868 — a resident of Stockport from mid-1961. Both engines were condemned when the shed closed. Photograph by David Christie.

Opposite page STOCKPORT EDGELEY STATION

BR introduced the Standard Class 9F 2-10-0 design in 1954 to move heavy freight trains around the country quickly. Some 251 locomotives were built up to early 1961 and worked across the regions. Here, no. 92047 heads an up oil tanker train through Stockport Edgeley station on 10th August 1967. The locomotive was erected at Crewe Works in February 1955 and was initially allocated to Loughborough shed but left at the end of the year for Bidston, Wirral. No. 92047 remained there until February 1963 when switching to Birkenhead and was withdrawn from the shed in November 1967. One of the principal duties of engines allocated there was the oil traffic from Stanlow Refinery, Ellesmere Port, to places such as Leeds, Nottingham, Birmingham and Carlisle. Photograph by Bill Wright.

Above STOCKPORT EDGELEY STATION

The pioneer Stanier locomotive and first LMSR Pacific, 'Princess Royal' Class no. 46200 *The Princess Royal* is at Stockport Edgeley station with the Plymouth to Manchester London Road express on 31st July 1950. Photograph by B.W.L. Brooksbank.

Below STOCKPORT EDGELEY STATION

An up local freight is headed by ex-LNWR Beames G2 Class 0-8-0 no. 49418 at Stockport Edgeley station on 19th June 1957. Photograph by B.W.L. Brooksbank.

Above STOCKPORT EDGELEY STATION

The 10.20 local service between Buxton and Manchester London Road has stopped at platform three, Stockport Edgeley, on 26th March 1955. The locomotive is Fowler 4P 2-6-4T no. 42363. Photograph by B.W.L. Brooksbank.

Below STOCKPORT EDGELEY STATION

This modest Fowler 4F was unique under BR in being the only locomotive in service with five identical digits — no. 44444 — although before Nationalisation four identical digits was relatively common. The engine is shunting wagons at the south end of Stockport Edgeley station on 31st July 1950. Photograph by B.W.L. Brooksbank.

Above TEBAY STATION

The North West of England was a particular safe haven for locomotives at the end of steam. Many 'Britannia' Class Pacifics congregated at Carlisle Kingmoor, given their ample power, robust design and relatively recent introduction. No. 70035 *Rudyard Kipling*, is at Tebay station with a freight train on 23rd June 1967, arrived at Carlisle in December 1963 and was condemned there in December 1967. Photograph by David Christie.

Above TEBAY STATION

BR Standard Class 4 no. 75030 was a recent addition to the ranks at Tebay shed for banking duties and arrived in early June 1967. The engine has been captured at the station on the 23rd June; no. 75030 would be withdrawn at the end of the year. Photograph by David Christie.

Below TEBAY SHED

BR Standard Class 4 no. 75026 and Stanier Class 5 no. 45253 are in the shed yard at Tebay on 20th October 1967. The shed was closed at the end of the year and resident no. 75026 was condemned at the same time. Photograph by Geoff Warnes.

Above TRAFFORD PARK SHED

Opened by the Cheshire Lines Committee in early 1895, Trafford Park shed, Manchester, was almost exactly 73 years old when visited here on 2nd March 1968 and due for closure in just two days time. Two dead and withdrawn engines are under cover, both Stanier Class 5s: no. 45257 (left) and no. 44895. Photograph by David Christie.

Below THRIMBY

Just north of Shap at Thrimby on the WCML, Standard Class 4 no. 75024 is with two brake vans on 23rd June 1967. Photograph by David Christie.

Above WARRINGTON
Approaching Folly Lane bridge, Warrington, from the south on 3rd May 1965 is BR Standard Class 9F no. 92126. The locomotive, which is at the head of a soda ash train from ICI Winnington, was a recent addition to Warrington Dallam shed (seen partially on the right) and would be condemned there in August 1967. Photograph by B.W.L. Brooksbank.

Below WARRINGTON BANK QUAY STATION
Only passing through Warrington Bank Quay station — under the alert gaze of a group of 'spotters' — on 17th August 1963 is Stanier Class 5 no. 45426. The train is 09.04 Stoke-on-Trent to Blackpool North. Photograph by B.W.L. Brooksbank.

Above WARRINGTON

A set of carriages appear to be undergoing a final clean and inspection from a female worker at Warrington Bank Quay sidings on 7th May 1965 before being taken out by Fowler 4P Class 2-6-4T no. 42369. Photograph by B.W.L. Brooksbank.

Below WIDNES SHED

On 25th March 1956, an unidentified ex-LNWR Cooke 0-8-0 stands outside Widnes Shed. Photograph by Geoff Warnes.

Above WORKINGTON SHED
Ivatt Class 2MT 2-6-0 no. 46459 is in the yard at Workington shed on 11th August 1951 before working a Penrith to Cockermouth service. Photograph by B.W.L. Brooksbank.

Below WORKINGTON SHED
Ex-LNWR Webb 18 in. Goods 'Cauliflower' 0-6-0 no. 58396 is at Workington shed on 13th August 1951. Photograph by B.W.L. Brooksbank.

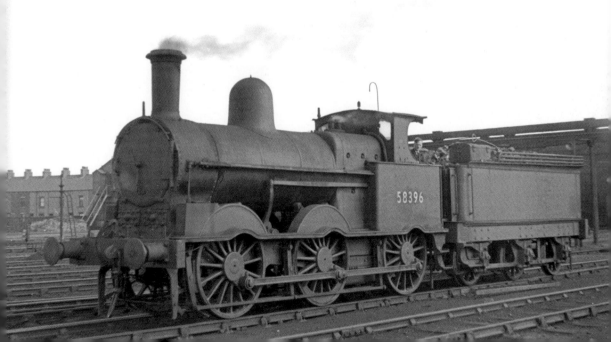

Above WIGAN NORTH WESTERN STATION
The up 'Caledonian' (Glasgow Central to Euston) speeds through Wigan North Western on 20th June 1957; 'Coronation' Pacific no. 46242 *City of Glasgow* is at the head. Photograph by B.W.L. Brooksbank.

Below WIGAN SPRINGS BRANCH SHED
Stanier 2-6-0 no. 42959 visits Wigan Springs Branch shed for servicing on 5th April 1959. The engine was allocated to Crewe at this time, but would move to Wigan in December 1963 and was condemned there two years later. Photograph by Geoff Warnes.

Above WIGAN NORTH WESTERN STATION
Stanier 8F no. 48646 has not been entrusted with working a passenger service from Wigan North Western station on 12th March 1968 as the carriages are empty and being worked to Edge Hill. Photograph by Bill Wright.

Below WIGAN SPRINGS BRANCH SHED
With the closure of Lower Ince shed in 1952, ex-GCR engines were transferred to Springs Branch. One was Pollitt 9H (LNER J10) Class 0-6-0 no. 65140, which stands amongst ex-LNWR and LMSR designs in the yard on 5th April 1959. Photograph by Geoff Warnes.

Above YANWATH

Just south of Penrith lies the village of Yanwath and the WCML passes by on the western side. The B5320 road bridge provides the vantage point for this shot of an unidentified Stanier Class 5 travelling northward on 12th September 1966. Photograph by David Christie.

Below YANWATH

Running tender-first southward at Yanwath on 12th September 1966 is Ivatt Class 4MT 2-6-0 no. 43029; the engine had just a year left in traffic. Photograph by David Christie.

Above YANWATH

Carlisle Kingmoor-allocated Stanier Class 5 no. 44669 speeds past Yanwath on the way northward to Penrith on 12th September 1966. The engine resided at the depot throughout the BR period and was condemned there in October 1967. Photograph by David Christie.

Below YANWATH

Another of Carlisle Kingmoor's long-term residents — Stanier Class 5 no. 44898 — heads south at Yanwath with a mixed freight service on 12th September 1966. Photograph by David Christie.

BIBLIOGRAPHY

Allen, C.J. *Titled Trains of Great Britain.* 1983.

Baker, Allan C. *The Book of the Coronation Pacifics Mk2.* 2010.

Christiansen, R. *Rail Centres: No. 19 – Crewe.* 2007.

Griffiths, Roger and Paul Smith. *The Directory of British Engine Sheds and Principal Locomotive Servicing Points: 2 North Midlands, Northern England and Scotland.* 2000.

Haresnape, Brian. *Fowler Locomotives.* 1997.

Haresnape, Brian. *Stanier Locomotives.* 1974.

Hawkins, Chris and George Reeve. *LMS Engine Sheds: Volume Two The Midland Railway.* 1981.

Hawkins, Chris and George Reeve. *LMS Engine Sheds: Volume Five The Caledonian Railway.* 1987.

Hunt, David, John Jennison, Fred James and Bob Essery. *LMS Locomotive Profiles: No. 5 – The Mixed Traffic Class 5s Nos 5000-5224.* 2003.

Hunt, David, John Jennison, Fred James and Bob Essery. *LMS Locomotive Profiles: No. 6 – The Mixed Traffic Class 5s Nos 5225-5499 and 4658-4999.* 2004.

Hunt, David, John Jennison, Fred James and Bob Essery. *LMS Locomotive Profiles: No. 7 – The Mixed Traffic Class 5s Caprotti Valve Gear Engines and Class Summary.* 2006.

Hunt, David, John Jennison, Fred James and Bob Essery. *LMS Locomotive Profiles: No. 8 – The Class 8F 2-8-0s.* 2005.

Larkin, Edgar. *An Illustrated History of British Railways' Workshops.* 2007.

Quick, Michael. *Railway Passenger Stations in Great Britain: A Chronology.* 2009.

RCTS. *A Detailed History of British Railways Standard Steam Locomotives: Volume One Background to Standardisation and the Pacific Classes.* 2007.

RCTS. *A Detailed History of British Railways Standard Steam Locomotives: Volume Four The 9F 2-10-0 Class.* 2008.

Robinson, Peter W. *Rail Centres: No. 6 – Carlisle.* 2004.

Sixsmith, Ian. *The Book of the Ivatt LM Class 4 2-6-0s.* 2012.

Townsin, Ray. *The Jubilee 4-6-0s.* 2006.

Walmsley, Tony. *Shed by Shed: Part One London Midland.* 2010.

Young, John and David Tyreman. *The Hughes and Stanier 2-6-0s.* 2009.

Also available from Great Northern by Peter Tuffrey

The Last Days of Scottish Steam

The Last Years of Yorkshire Steam

The Golden Age of Yorkshire Railways

Gresley's A3s

Peppercorn's Pacifics

London Midland Steam 1948-1966

The Last Years of North East Steam

British Railways Standard Pacifics

Western Steam 1948-1966

visit *www.greatnorthernbooks.co.uk* for details.